CAPTURING CARBON
WITH FAKE TREES

BY CECILIA PINTO McCARTHY

CONTENT CONSULTANT
Xiaoyang Shi
Post-Doctoral Research Associate, Earth and Environmental
Engineering, Columbia University

Cover image: This huge air purifier turns carbon
into diamonds.

Core Library

An Imprint of Abdo Publishing
abdobooks.com

abdocorelibrary.com

Published by Abdo Publishing, a division of ABDO, PO Box 398166,
Minneapolis, Minnesota 55439. Copyright © 2020 by Abdo Consulting
Group, Inc. International copyrights reserved in all countries. No part of this
book may be reproduced in any form without written permission from the
publisher. Core Library™ is a trademark and logo of Abdo Publishing.

Printed in the United States of America, North Mankato, Minnesota
042019
092019

**THIS BOOK CONTAINS
RECYCLED MATERIALS**

Cover Photo: Chen junmin/Imaginechina/AP Images
Interior Photos: Chen junmin/Imaginechina/AP Images, 1; Ari Daniel, 4–5, 7, 34–35; Everett
Historical/Shutterstock Images, 9, 43; Leighton Collins/Shutterstock Images, 10; iStockphoto,
14–15, 17; Shutterstock Images, 20; Chesnot/Getty Images News/Getty Images, 22; Climeworks/
Julia Dunlop/Cover Images/Newscom, 24–25; Red Line Editorial, 26; Melanie Stetson Freeman/The
Christian Science Monitor/Getty Images, 27, 31, 45; Saul Loeb/AFP/Getty Images, 36

Editor: Marie Pearson
Series Designer: Ryan Gale

Library of Congress Control Number: 2018966158

Publisher's Cataloging-in-Publication Data

Names: McCarthy, Cecilia Pinto, author.
Title: Capturing carbon with fake trees / by Cecilia Pinto McCarthy
Description: Minneapolis, Minnesota : Abdo Publishing, 2020 | Series: Unconventional science |
    Includes online resources and index.
Identifiers: ISBN 9781532118968 (lib. bdg.) | ISBN 9781532173141 (ebook) |
    ISBN 9781644940877 (pbk.)
Subjects: LCSH: Climate change mitigation--Juvenile literature. | Atmospheric carbon dioxide
    mitigation--Juvenile literature. | Carbon offsetting--Juvenile literature. | Environmental
    protection--Juvenile literature. | Air pollution control--Juvenile literature.
Classification: DDC 363.738747--dc23

CONTENTS

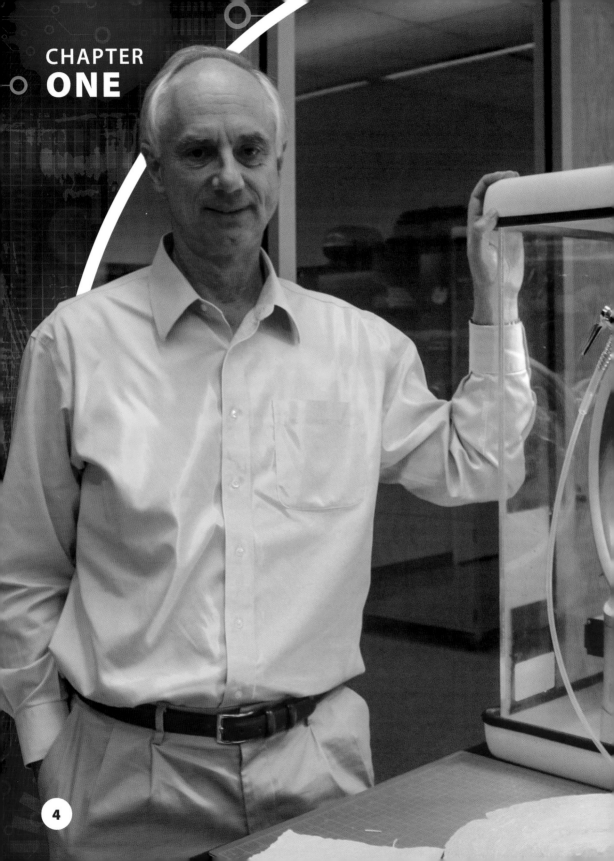

CONTROLLING CARBON

D r. Klaus Lackner teaches at Arizona State University. He is giving a demonstration in his laboratory. A large, clear box sits on a table. The box is a sealed greenhouse. Inside the box are several plants. Lackner opens a round door on the box. He places a square of material inside. The material looks like a piece of shaggy white rug. Lackner locks the airtight door. Next, he turns to watch a monitor attached to the greenhouse. The monitor shows the amount of carbon dioxide inside the greenhouse. Immediately, the carbon dioxide levels begin to rise.

Klaus Lackner's greenhouse allows him to test carbon-capture technology.

Carbon dioxide is a gas. As plants grow, they take in carbon dioxide from the air. They use the gas to make food. The plants in Lackner's sealed greenhouse cannot get carbon dioxide from the air. Yet they are thriving. They get carbon dioxide from the shaggy square that Lackner places in the greenhouse.

ABSORBING CARBON

The square is made of plastic. Some of the plastic helps the square keep its shape. It also holds tiny pieces of a special plastic called resin. This resin can grab molecules from a liquid or gas. When it's

A WINNING IDEA

Klaus Lackner's daughter Claire inspired his idea for capturing carbon. As a middle school student, Claire made an experiment to pull carbon dioxide from the air. She used sodium hydroxide. The chemical absorbs carbon dioxide. Claire filled a test tube with the chemical. Then she used an air pump to force air into the tube. The sodium hydroxide absorbed the carbon dioxide from the air. Claire entered her experiment in the science fair. She won first prize. Lackner began experimenting with capturing carbon himself.

Lackner's carbon-capture material can be made in different shapes.

dry, this resin absorbs carbon dioxide. But when the

resin gets wet, it releases the gas. Lackner's resin

absorbed carbon dioxide from air in the lab. Inside the

greenhouse, humid air made the resin wet. The resin then released its carbon dioxide. The resin has another important characteristic. It is reusable. The same piece of material can be used repeatedly to absorb and release carbon dioxide.

GREENHOUSE GASES

Lackner and his team want to capture carbon dioxide from Earth's atmosphere. Currently the atmosphere contains too much of the gas. Carbon dioxide is a type of greenhouse gas. Greenhouse gases absorb heat. Like the roof on a greenhouse, these gases hold heat in the atmosphere above Earth. Greenhouse gases are important. They keep the planet warm. Life would not be possible without them.

But since the Industrial Revolution, greenhouse gas levels have been rising. The Industrial Revolution began in the mid-1700s. Since then, machines, factories, and vehicles have been burning coal, oil, and other fuels.

Factories and machines add a lot of greenhouse gases to the air.

The fuels release large amounts of carbon dioxide into the atmosphere.

The extra carbon dioxide traps too much heat. It causes Earth's temperatures to rise. Since the beginning of the Industrial Revolution, Earth has warmed approximately 1.8 degrees Fahrenheit (1°C). This rise is called climate change. There are signs of climate change around the world. Glaciers and ice caps are melting. Sea levels are rising. There are more extreme weather events. These events cause damage worldwide.

CAPTURING CARBON WITH FAKE TREES

Fake trees are one solution to too much carbon dioxide. Fake trees usually do not look like real trees. But like real trees, they capture carbon dioxide. They capture the gas directly from the air. Lackner imagines making forests of fake trees. The forests will reduce carbon dioxide in the air.

Powerful storms are growing more common as Earth's temperature rises.

MANY METHODS

Many technologies help fight climate change. One group of technologies is carbon dioxide removal (CDR). CDR includes fake trees. Other types of CDR are machines. These are used in industrial and power plants. The devices grab carbon dioxide and other pollutants before they are released. Solar radiation management (SRM) is another type. SRM reflects sunlight into space. Both of these technologies are controversial. Some experts think interfering with the environment may cause problems. SRM does not lower the level of carbon dioxide near Earth's surface. And CDR can use a lot of energy.

People are still working on fake-tree technology. Several companies are testing the technology. Researchers are looking for ways to make the trees more efficient. Fake trees may be common in the future.

STRAIGHT TO THE
SOURCE

The 2015 Paris climate agreement is a global agreement. It calls on nations to fight climate change. Writer Rebecca Harrington explains the agreement:

> *The Paris Agreement was designed to keep the planet from warming by more than 1.5 degrees Celsius [2.7°F] above preindustrial levels. . . .*
>
> *Climate experts say that an increase of more than 2 degrees Celsius [3.6°F] in the planet's temperature could bring about irreversible consequences, including a rise in sea level, superstorms, and crippling heat waves. It was estimated in 2011 that the average global surface temperature was increasing at a rate of more than 0.1 degree Celsius [0.18°F] a decade.*

> Source: Rebecca Harrington. "Here's What the US Actually Agreed To in the Paris Climate Deal," *Business Insider*. Business Insider, June 1, 2017. Web. Accessed October 30, 2018.

Consider Your Audience

Read the passage carefully. Adapt this passage for a different audience, such as your parents or friends. Write a blog post conveying this same information for the new audience. How does your post differ from the original text and why?

Junction I-225   1
Belleview Ave   1¼
Orchard Road   3

THE CARBON CYCLE

Plants, animals, land, oceans, and rocks all contain carbon. Carbon is also in fossil fuels. These fuels formed from plants and animals that died millions of years ago. Their remains were buried under layers of soil and rock. Heat and pressure changed the remains into fossil fuels. Fossil fuels contain carbon from the bodies. Coal, oil, and natural gas are types of fossil fuels.

ON THE MOVE

Carbon is always moving. It flows between organisms, rocks, the air, land, and oceans. This movement is called the carbon cycle. This cycle

Most cars run on gasoline, a form of fossil fuel.

can be fast or slow. Carbon moves quickly through organisms on Earth. Plants play a major role in the fast cycle. They take in carbon dioxide from the air. Trees store most of the carbon in their trunks and branches. Tree roots move some carbon into underground soil. If left undisturbed, carbon can stay in soil for one thousand years. Carbon can cycle through both plants and animals in a few ways. An animal may eat a plant. The carbon in the plant moves to the animal. In the animal's body, carbon mixes with oxygen. This forms carbon dioxide. Carbon dioxide is released into the air when the animal breathes. Carbon also moves when plants and animals die. Bacteria and fungi break down the remains. This releases carbon into the soil.

Some carbon moves to rocks, oceans, and fossil fuels. It moves slowly. It can stay in place for millions of years. Volcanic activity may release stored carbon. Burning fossil fuel also releases carbon. The released carbon mixes with oxygen in the air. It forms carbon dioxide.

THE CARBON CYCLE

This diagram shows how carbon moves between the air, ocean, and land. What processes add carbon to the air? What processes absorb carbon dioxide from the air?

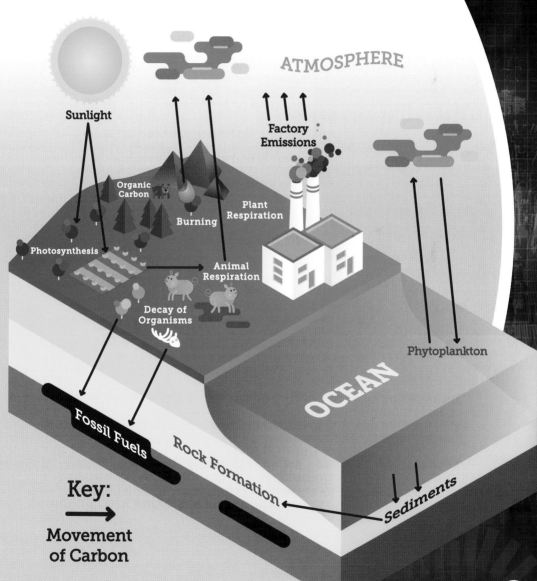

CARBON SINKS

Forests, oceans, and soil are carbon sinks. They absorb and store carbon dioxide. Trees take in and store carbon dioxide in their trunks and roots. Some carbon is moved to and stored in the soil. When trees die and decompose, their carbon is released. Oceans absorb carbon dioxide from the air. About one-quarter of the extra carbon dioxide added by human activity dissolves in the ocean. But rising temperatures are causing carbon sinks to become carbon sources. Warmer temperatures make plants break down faster and release more carbon. Warm water currents bring deep-water carbon up to the ocean's surface. Then it is released into the air.

AN UNBALANCED CYCLE

The carbon cycle keeps carbon dioxide levels balanced. Systems that store carbon, such as rocks and oceans, are linked. When carbon levels in one system change, so do the levels in other systems.

Human activities have added extra carbon dioxide to the cycle. Now the cycle is off balance. Fossil fuels deep underground release carbon slowly. But when burned, they give off carbon dioxide quickly. Clearing trees from forests also adds carbon dioxide to the air. There are fewer trees to take in carbon dioxide. Carbon is also released when trees decay or are burned.

For many years, scientists have warned about climate change. Too much carbon dioxide is changing the planet. Some of the carbon dioxide goes into the ocean. It is making oceans acidic. Acidic water softens the shells of mussels and oysters. It kills coral reefs. Warm temperatures are melting Arctic ice. The added water is causing sea levels to rise. Coastal flooding has become common. Plants and animals are losing habitats. There are powerful storms, droughts, and forest fires around the world.

A CALL TO ACTION

In 2015, countries signed the Paris climate agreement. They agreed to cut carbon emissions. The aim was to limit Earth's warming to less than 3.6 degrees Fahrenheit (2°C). Ideally, the temperature rise wouldn't

get more than 2.7 degrees Fahrenheit (1.5°C) over the levels before the Industrial Revolution. The agreement set a target date of 2050.

In October 2018, the United Nations Intergovernmental Panel on Climate Change (IPCC) released a report. It found that a 1.8 degrees Fahrenheit (1°C) rise in global temperature is causing changes. Sea levels are rising. There is more extreme weather. Arctic sea ice is melting. The report says that many climate change effects can

MEASURING CARBON

In 1958, Charles Keeling worked for the Scripps Institution of Oceanography. He began measuring carbon dioxide levels in the air. The daily measurements were taken at the top of Hawaiian volcano Mauna Loa and at the South Pole. Keeling noticed that carbon dioxide levels varied with the seasons. Also, the average concentration of carbon dioxide was rising. The concentration across the years is now plotted on a graph called the Keeling curve.

Things like warmer water temperatures put coral under stress, making it turn white in a process called bleaching.

The Eiffel Tower in Paris, France, lit up with messages supporting cutting emissions at the time of the Paris climate agreement.

be prevented if climate change is kept to 2.7 degrees Fahrenheit (1.5°C). Accomplishing this goal requires immediate action. People will need to limit their use of fossil fuels. By 2030, emissions from human activity need to be cut in half. They would have to be eliminated by 2050.

CARBON NEUTRALITY

Achieving net zero carbon emissions is known as carbon neutrality. The amount of carbon released is balanced by the same amount of carbon captured. This is a hard goal to reach. Most technologies are powered by fossil fuels. Other power sources such as solar and wind energy do not provide enough energy to meet the demand. These sources are also more expensive than fossil fuels. If temperatures rise above the IPCC target, the world will need to pull carbon from the air. Fake trees could be one solution.

FURTHER EVIDENCE

Chapter Two discusses how carbon dioxide levels in the air are rising. What was one of the main points of this chapter? What evidence supports this point? Read the article at the website below. Does it support the main point of the chapter? Does it present new evidence?

CAUSES OF GLOBAL WARMING
abdocorelibrary.com/fake-trees-capture-carbon

DIRECT AIR CAPTURE TECHNOLOGY

I f nothing is done, carbon levels will keep rising. Before the Industrial Revolution, the concentration of carbon dioxide in the air was approximately 275 parts per million (ppm). Experts think that carbon must be kept at or below 350 ppm to control climate change. But in 2018, the daily average was more than 400 ppm.

Direct air capture (DAC) can remove carbon dioxide. DAC collects carbon dioxide from air near the ground. The carbon dioxide

Direct air capture technology pulls carbon dioxide from the air.

ATMOSPHERIC
CARBON
DIOXIDE

This graph shows the average level of carbon dioxide in the atmosphere measured at the Mauna Loa Observatory by year. How much did the level of carbon dioxide rise between 1965 and 2000?

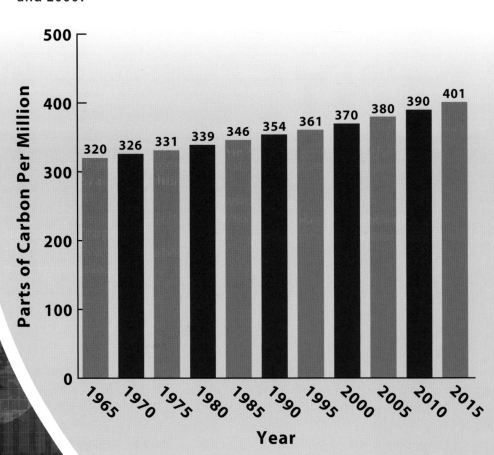

Some DAC technology sends carbon to special sites to be injected into the ground.

can then be stored. It can also be reused. DAC devices are sometimes called fake trees.

DAC already removes carbon dioxide inside spacecraft and submarines. But capturing carbon from the open air is harder. DAC uses a three-step process. First, air flows through a special area in a DAC device.

There, a chemical pulls the carbon from the air. Then that carbon is purified. It can be stored underground. Some companies use it to make fuels. Others sell it to companies that make soft drinks. Carbon is what gives soft drinks their fizz.

DESIGNING DAC

Klaus Lackner is a pioneer in DAC. He sees carbon emissions as trash dumped into the air. He thinks fake trees can clean this waste from the air. Lackner has built a full-sized working model of a fake tree. It uses filters that absorb carbon. The filters are made of sheets. The sheets open and fold like a sail. When open and dry, the sheets absorb carbon dioxide. When wet, the sheets release

NATURAL METHODS

There are several ways to pull carbon dioxide from the air. Some include using fake trees. But natural processes can also reduce carbon. These include reforestation. Reforestation involves planting many trees. The trees capture carbon in their wood. They move some of the carbon to the soil.

the gas. This process does use water, which is not always readily available.

Another of Lackner's designs looks like a large tuning fork. The U-shaped device stands on a central post. Filter sheets hang down and act like leaves. As wind blows air over the sheets, they bind carbon dioxide. The sheets fill with carbon dioxide in 45 minutes to 1 hour. Once the filters are full, they are taken down and put in a box. Water is added to the box, and the filters release the carbon dioxide. The wet leaves are hung outside to dry. Then they begin collecting carbon again.

Fake trees are 1,000 times faster at capturing carbon than real trees. They remove extra carbon in the air. A fake tree the size of a trailer truck can collect approximately 1 short ton (0.9 metric tons) of carbon dioxide a day. Lackner estimates it would take 100 million fake trees to capture the carbon emissions being given off each year.

CARBON-CAPTURE COMPANIES

In 2017, a Swiss company called Climeworks started the first commercial carbon-capture facility. It is in Zurich, Switzerland. The carbon captured at the plant is sold to a nearby greenhouse. The added carbon increases the crop harvest by 20 to 30 percent. The Climeworks facility runs on energy it gets from a waste burning plant next door.

Climeworks's equipment is made up of units. The units are called contactors. A fan on each contactor pulls in air. Carbon dioxide from the air sticks to a filter. When the filter is full, it is heated to 212°F (100°C). The heat releases the carbon dioxide from the filter. The gas is then collected.

Climeworks contactor units are modular. Units can be put together in sets. A facility with more units captures more carbon. Carbon-capture plants can be made with 1, 3, 18, or 36 units.

Some Climeworks contactors are used in Iceland.

STORING CARBON

Long-term carbon storage is called sequestration. Carbon can be naturally stored in plants, soil, rocks, and the ocean. Captured carbon can be stored underground. It is pumped 0.6 to 2.5 miles (1–4 km) below the ground's surface. It can be injected into rock formations. Eventually, some of the carbon dioxide dissolves in water. It may react with rocks and form minerals. Scientists are studying the possible risks of underground storage. Gas pressure may cause tremors. Carbon dioxide may leak into the air or contaminate water. Experts think that these events are unlikely.

Another company is based in New York. Global Thermostat makes tower-shaped contactors. The units have a honeycomb design. They are portable. Global Thermostat's focus is on capturing carbon dioxide from power plants and other industries. They capture carbon dioxide before it is released into the air.

CARBON ENGINEERING

The Carbon Engineering (CE)

company is in British Columbia, Canada. It uses a four-step process to collect carbon. First, chemicals capture carbon dioxide. The carbon dioxide is then formed into solid pellets. When the pellets are heated, they break apart. This forms a powder. The powder releases purified carbon dioxide. CE recycles some of the captured carbon dioxide. It uses the gas to make fuel. The fuel does release some carbon dioxide when burned. But it burns cleaner than fossil fuels.

EXPLORE ONLINE

Chapter Three talks about direct air capture of carbon dioxide. The video at the website below also discusses direct air capture. How is the information from the website the same as the information in Chapter Three? What new information did you learn from the website?

ASU RESEARCH: CARBON FARMING
abdocorelibrary.com/fake-trees-capture-carbon

THE FUTURE OF FAKE TREES

D AC is making positive strides. But its future is uncertain. Researchers have proven that DAC is possible. DAC devices have become easy to transport. They can meet the needs of different industries. But despite DAC's advantages, its progress has been slow.

CHALLENGES

Cost has been stalling the progress of fake trees. Research, development, and construction of DAC machines is expensive. One reason for the cost is that pulling carbon dioxide from air is hard. Only 0.04 percent of air is carbon dioxide. To capture enough of

Scientists are inventing many kinds of carbon-capture technology. Some look like cubes.

Computer programs help monitor the collection and storage of carbon.

the gas, DAC contactors need large surface areas. Large machines are expensive to build. In 2011, the American Physical Society released a report on DAC technology. It estimated that it would cost $600 or more to capture 1 short ton (0.9 metric tons) of carbon dioxide. Other estimates put the cost at $1,000 per ton of carbon dioxide. It would take thousands of DAC devices to make much progress. That many machines would also take up a lot of space.

Lackner's fake trees face the same obstacle. One fake tree costs approximately $300,000. So building the necessary 100 million fake trees would be very expensive. Operating so many fake trees is also costly. The trees use a lot of water and electricity. Even if fake trees become cheaper to build, it will take a long time to make and place millions of trees around the world.

Some people also worry that building DAC plants might produce more carbon. The materials and the building process use machines. These machines use fossil fuels. DAC plants could add more carbon than they remove.

A POSITIVE STEP FORWARD

Lackner and other researchers think that DAC manufacturing costs will eventually be reduced. They expect costs to fall as experts perfect DAC devices and processes. The challenge is to make and run devices cheaply, efficiently, and effectively. Companies also need to manufacture enough trees to reduce the amount of carbon dioxide in the air. DAC units are a step in the right direction.

In June 2018, the company Carbon Engineering (CE) reported that it had greatly reduced the cost of removing carbon dioxide. Its estimate is between $94 and $232 to remove 1 short ton (0.9 metric tons) of carbon dioxide. These numbers are based on

GROWING FOOD WITH DAC

New York company Infinitree is solving two issues through DAC. Its technology is called Humidity Swing Technology. The devices attach to greenhouses. Carbon dioxide is absorbed from the air outside the greenhouse. Humidity created by plants in the greenhouse releases the carbon dioxide. The gas flows into the greenhouse. The plants can then use it. Adding carbon dioxide to the greenhouse boosts plant growth. It allows plants to grow all year. Carbon dioxide-fed greenhouses can be used to grow food in cities.

CE's plant in Canada. There, some of the carbon is processed into low-carbon fuels and sold. Selling fuels helps offset the cost of the carbon-capture process. CE's progress is good news. But only time will tell if it is successful. Even if the company's estimates are right, the overall cost of carbon capture is still high. CE is still unsure if it can build plants that will greatly cut carbon dioxide levels.

THE VIRGIN EARTH CHALLENGE

English businessman Sir Richard Branson started the Virgin Earth Challenge in 2007. Branson wanted to inspire the development of carbon-capture technology. The winning design must be a device that can be commercially produced. The device must be able to remove large amounts of carbon dioxide each year. It must run for at least ten years. The winner will receive a prize of $25 million. Out of 10,000 applications, 11 companies have been chosen as finalists. Those finalists include CE, Climeworks, and Global Thermostat. The final prize will be awarded to the company that creates a commercially successful solution.

DAC companies like CE are trying to balance manufacturing costs by selling their captured carbon. They are partnering with industries that need carbon to manufacture goods. Greenhouses, beverage companies, and oil companies all use carbon dioxide. Selling carbon dioxide may help make DAC profitable. The profits can be used to build more DAC facilities.

Fake trees alone will not solve climate change. The need to advance DAC technology and combat climate change has become more urgent. DAC, along with other methods, must be part of the plan to reduce carbon dioxide. If DAC is to succeed, it will need the support of scientists, governments, and the public.

STRAIGHT TO THE
SOURCE

Scientists around the world are researching ways to limit climate change. Peter Wadhams, professor of ocean physics at the University of Cambridge, discusses the challenge:

> We now emit 41 billion tons of carbon dioxide per year. . . . We must either reduce our emissions to zero, which is not yet possible, or combine a significant emissions reduction with the physical removal of about 20 billion [metric] tons [22 billion short tons] of carbon dioxide from the atmosphere per year indefinitely. . . .
>
> Currently, the best way to save our future is to remove carbon dioxide through direct air capture. . . .
>
> If we can manage this, we can save our society and our children's futures.

> Source: Peter Wadhams. "Saving the World with Carbon Dioxide Removal," *Washington Post*. Washington Post, January 8, 2018. Web. Accessed October 30, 2018.

What's the Big Idea?
Take a close look at this passage. What does the writer think must be done to combat excess carbon dioxide in the air?

FAST FACTS

- Since the Industrial Revolution, carbon dioxide levels in the atmosphere have been rising.

- Carbon dioxide is a greenhouse gas.

- Greenhouse gases act as a blanket that holds in heat in Earth's atmosphere.

- Cars, trucks, ships, and industrial machines and processes add excess carbon dioxide to the atmosphere.

- The planet is warming because of growing levels of greenhouse gases.

- The carbon cycle describes the constant flow of carbon between organisms, rocks, air, land, and oceans.

- Fake trees are a type of direct air capture (DAC) technology.

- Fake trees are devices that absorb carbon dioxide from the air.

- Absorbed carbon dioxide can be stored underground. It can also be used to make products.

- DAC technology has been developed on a small scale.

- The development of fake trees is still expensive.

- More funding is needed to build carbon-capture devices on a large scale.

- Fake trees must be used along with other methods to combat climate change.

STOP AND THINK

Tell the Tale

Chapter Three of this book discusses Klaus Lackner's work designing fake trees. Imagine that you are an assistant in Lackner's laboratory. Write 200 words about the carbon-capture experiments you are carrying out. Do you have an idea for the design of a fake tree?

Surprise Me

Chapter Two discusses the carbon cycle. After reading this book, what two or three facts about carbon did you find most surprising? Write a few sentences about each fact. Why did you find each fact surprising?

Dig Deeper

After reading this book, what questions do you still have about capturing carbon with fake trees? With an adult's help, find a few reliable sources that can help you answer your questions. Write a paragraph about what you learned.

Say What?

Studying fake trees and direct air capture can mean learning a lot of new vocabulary. Find five words in this book you've never heard before. Use a dictionary to find out what they mean. Then write the meanings in your own words and use each word in a new sentence.

GLOSSARY

atmosphere
the layer of gases
surrounding a planet

climate
the average varying weather
conditions in a certain region

commercial
made to sell for a profit

emission
the production and discharge
of something, such as gases
from a car

industrial
having to do with industry

industry
groups that make related
items and sell them for profit

modular
using units in a set to
construct something

molecule
the smallest unit of a
chemical compound that
still has all the properties of
that chemical

pioneer
someone who leads the way
in a new field or technology

purified
cleansed; having gotten rid
of impurities

ONLINE RESOURCES

To learn more about capturing carbon with fake trees, visit our free resource websites below.

Visit **abdocorelibrary.com** or scan this QR code for free Common Core resources for teachers and students, including vetted activities, multimedia, and booklinks, for deeper subject comprehension.

Visit **abdobooklinks.com** or scan this QR code for free additional online weblinks for further learning. These links are routinely monitored and updated to provide the most current information available.

LEARN MORE

Gagne, Tammy. *Rain Forest Ecosystems*. Minneapolis, MN: Abdo Publishing, 2016. Print.

Steele, Philip. *Analyzing Climate Change*. New York: Cavendish Square Publishing, 2019. Print.

INDEX

About the Author

Cecilia Pinto McCarthy has written several children's
books about science and nature. She also teaches classes
at a nature sanctuary. She and her family live north of
Boston, Massachusetts.